CENGAGE Learning

Drama for Students, Volume 13

Staff

Editor: Elizabeth Thomason.

Contributing Editors: Reginald Carlton, Anne Marie Hacht, Michael L. LaBlanc, Ira Mark Milne, Jennifer Smith.

Managing Editor, Content: Dwayne D. Hayes.

Managing Editor, Product: David Galens.

Publisher, Literature Product: Mark Scott.

Literature Content Capture: Joyce Nakamura, *Managing Editor.* Michelle Poole, *Associate Editor.*

Research: Victoria B. Cariappa, *Research Manager.* Cheryl Warnock, *Research Specialist.* Tamara Nott, Tracie A. Richardson, *Research Associates.* Nicodemus Ford, Sarah Genik, Timothy Lehnerer, Ron Morelli, *Research Assistants.*

Permissions: Maria Franklin, *Permissions*

Manager. Debra J. Freitas, Jacqueline Jones, Julie Juengling, *Permissions Assistants*.

Manufacturing: Mary Beth Trimper, *Manager, Composition and Electronic Prepress*. Evi Seoud, *Assistant Manager, Composition Purchasing and Electronic Prepress*. Stacy Melson, *Buyer*.

Imaging and Multimedia Content Team: Barbara Yarrow, *Manager*. Randy Bassett, *Imaging Supervisor*. Robert Duncan, Dan Newell, *Imaging Specialists*. Pamela A. Reed, *Imaging Coordinator*. Leitha Etheridge-Sims, Mary Grimes, David G. Oblender, *Image Catalogers*. Robyn V. Young, *Project Manager*. Dean Dauphinais, *Senior Image Editor*. Kelly A. Quin, *Image Editor*.

Product Design Team: Kenn Zorn, *Product Design Manager*. Pamela A. E. Galbreath, *Senior Art Director*. Michael Logusz, *Graphic Artist*.

Copyright Notice

©2001 Gale Group
27500 Drake Rd.
Farmington Hills, MI 48331-3535

Gale Group and Design is a trademark used herein under license.

This book is printed on acid-free paper that meets the minimum requirements of American National Standard for Information Sciences—Permanence Paper for Printed Library Materials, ANSIZ39.48-1984.

ISBN 0-7876-4087-5
ISSN 1094-9232

Printed in the United States of America
10 9 8 7 6 5 4 3 2 1

Amadeus

Peter Shaffer 1979

Introduction

When Peter Shaffer's *Amadeus* opened at the National Theatre of Great Britain in November 1979, it was received enthusiastically by audiences and critics alike. One year after its premiere, London audiences began to line up at ticket offices at six in the morning on the day of performance. Shaffer revised the play extensively before its American debut in Washington, D.C., in November 1980. Soon after, the play opened on Broadway, where it won five Tonys, including a Tony for best drama of the 1980 season. The popularity of the play ensured the success of the 1984 film version, directed by Milos Forman, which received nominations for eleven Oscars and won eight, including best picture, best director, and best actor. *Amadeus* has also gained appreciative audiences internationally.

The play explores the rivalry between Wolfgang Amadeus Mozart and Antonio Salieri, the court composer for the Emperor of Austria in the late eighteenth century. Shaffer became interested in the relationship between the two composers after learning about Mozart's mysterious death. Although failing to find evidence that Salieri murdered Mozart, Shaffer admits, in an interview with Roland Gelatt, that "by then the cold eyes of Salieri were staring at me.... The conflict between virtuous mediocrity and feckless genius took hold of my imagination, and it would not leave me alone." Critics have praised the play's craftsmanship and its penetrating psychological study of the effects of success and failure and the search for spirituality.

Author Biography

Peter Shaffer and his twin brother, Anthony, were born in Liverpool, England, on May 15, 1926, to Jack (a real estate agent) and Reka (Fredman) Shaffer. When Shaffer was ten, the family moved to London, where Shaffer attended St. Paul's School. There he developed an interest in music, which would be a catalyst for his later treatment of the story of Mozart and Salieri in *Amadeus*.

After earning a degree from Cambridge in 1950, Shaffer moved to New York City and found employment at a book shop in the New York Public Library. When he relocated to London in 1954, he began writing scripts for radio and television. His first stage play, *Five Finger Exercise,* produced in 1958, won the New York Drama Critics Circle Award for best foreign play in 1960. *Royal Hunt of the Sun,* which opened in 1964, solidified his literary reputation. This play, which dramatizes the Spanish conquest of the Inca empire, focuses on explorations of success, humiliation, and faith— themes that Shaffer would return to in his later plays.

He gained more accolades for *Equus* (1973), which won the Antoinette Perry (Tony) Award and the New York Drama Critics Circle Award, and *Amadeus,* which won five Tony Awards in 1981 and was named best play of the year by *Plays and Players*. The film version of *Amadeus* won several

Academy Awards in 1984, including best picture and best screenplay adaptation for Shaffer's script. In 1994, Shaffer was appointed Cameron Mackintosh Visiting Professor of Contemporary Theatre at Oxford University.

Shaffer has been heralded for his successful work in a variety of dramatic genres, including comedy and domestic and historical drama, and for his compelling exploration of psychological themes.

Act 1

Amadeus opens with "savage whispers" that fill the theater. The citizens of Vienna in 1823 hiss the name "Salieri" and "assassin." Antonio Salieri, an old man, appears in a wheelchair, with his back to the audience. Two *venticelli,* "purveyors of fact, rumor and gossip throughout the play," hurry in, speaking rapidly about "the whole city... talking day and night." Salieri cries out, "Mozart! Pardon your assassin... have mercy." The *venticelli* explain that when Mozart died thirty-two years ago, there was some talk about him being poisoned by Salieri. They wonder why Salieri would do such a thing and why he would confess it now.

Salieri asks the audience to be his confessors. He admits his lifelong desire for fame, "yet only in one especial way. Music! Absolute music... music is God's art." He longed "to join all the composers who had celebrated His glory through the long Italian past." As a result, he implored God, "let me be a composer... in return, I will live with virtue... and I will honor You with much music all the days of my life." When God responded to him, "Go forth, Antonio. Serve Me and mankind, and you will be blessed," Salieri thanked him and promised, "I am Your servant for life."

The very next day, a family friend suddenly

appeared and took him to Vienna, where he studied music and soon became the court composer. Salieri decided, "Clearly my bargain had been accepted." The same year the young prodigy Mozart was touring Europe. Salieri tells the audience,' I present to you—for one performance only—my last composition, entitled *The Death of Mozart, or, Did I Do It?* dedicated to posterity on this, the last night of my life." He then takes off his dressing gown and becomes a young man wearing the elegant clothes of a successful composer in the 1780s.

The scene shifts to 1781 and Emperor Joseph II and his court in Vienna. Salieri is thirty-one, "a prolific" composer to the Hapsburg court, and married to "a respectable" wife, Teresa. The *venticelli,* Salieri's "Little Winds," announce that Mozart will be giving a concert for the court. While Salieri sits in a chair eating sweets in the library at the Palace of Schoönbrunn, Constanze Weber, daughter of Mozart's landlady, runs into the room squeaking like a mouse. Mozart follows her meowing like a cat. Mozart teases Constanze (Stanzi) with sexual innuendoes and bathroom humor and frequently emits "an unforgettable giggle—piercing and infantile." His demeanor appalls Salieri. Later, when Mozart begins playing one of his compositions, Salieri responds with such delight that it makes him tremble. He runs out into the street, "gasping for life." Addressing the audience, he explains, "it seemed to me that I had heard a voice of God. .. and it was the voice of an obscene child" After the conceit, Salieri buries his fear in work and prays to God, asking Him, "let

Your voice enter me!" When his "Little Winds" report that audiences seem unimpressed by Mozart's performances, Salieri begins to think that the serenade he heard was an exception, "an accident."

Salieri composes an "extremely banal" march in Mozart's honor. When Mozart quickly transforms it into an exceptional piece of music, Salieri admits, "was it then—so early—that I began to have thoughts of murder?" Mozart clashes with the emperor's advisors over his choice of subject and music for his commissioned operas. He also has difficulty finding pupils. Against the wishes of his father, he and Constanze marry and the two live well beyond their means. When Constanze asks Salieri to help her husband get work, the composer sees this as an opportunity to take his revenge. He invites her to his apartment, where he plans to seduce her. After Salieri makes it clear that he will help Mozart if she grants him sexual favors, she at first resists, but soon starts to tease him. Salieri then throws her out, offended by her "commonness" and angry at his own considered descent into adultery and blackmail.

When Salieri studies the manuscripts Constanze left behind, he hears the music in his head, acknowledging that they are the same sounds he had heard at the palace, "the same crushed harmonies—glancing collisions—agonizing delights." The piece he had heard "had been no accident." He admits, "I was staring through the cage of those meticulous ink strokes at—an

Absolute Beauty." As a result, he feels betrayed by God:

> I know my fate. Now for the first time I feel my emptiness as Adam felt his nakedness.... You gave me the desire to serve You... then saw to it the service was shameful in the ears of the server.... You gave me the desire to praise You... then made me mute.... You put into me perception of the Incomparable... then ensured that I would know myself forever mediocre.... MOZART!... spiteful, sniggering, conceited, infantine Mozart... him You have chosen to be Your sole conduct.

A bitter Salieri warns God, "From this time we are enemies, You and I. I'll not accept it from You —do you hear?... you are the Enemy. I name Thee now... and this I swear: to my last breath I shall block You on earth, as far as I am able."

The scene shifts to the present, with the older Salieri promising to reveal to the audience the details of "the war [he] fought with God through His preferred Creature—Mozart ... in the waging of which, of course, the Creature had to be destroyed."

Act 2

Back in the past, audiences are still not appreciating Mozart's work. His resulting desperation is compounded when his father dies. In an effort to earn money, he writes *The Magic Flute,* "something for ordinary German people." Salieri suggests he include in his composition a focus on the Masons, the fraternal order of which both are members. While he composes *The Magic Flute,* Constanze leaves with the children and his health deteriorates. He is continually taunted by dreams of a figure in gray, who compels him to write a requiem Mass.

When a member of the emperor's court discovers that Mozart has exposed Masonic rituals in *The Magic Flute,* he is outraged. As a result, Mozart's reputation and career are ruined. Soon after, when Mozart dies, Salieri admits to feeling a mixture of relief and pity. In the present, Salieri explains,

> Slowly I understood the nature of God's punishment.... This was my sentence: I must endure thirty years of being called "distinguished" by people incapable of distinguishing... and finally... when my nose had been rubbed in fame to vomiting—it would be taken away from me.... Mozart's music sounded louder and louder through the world. And mine faded completely, till no one played it at all.

Salieri admits he has attempted to convince the world that he poisoned Mozart, so that he will be remembered, "if not in fame, then infamy," and so win his battle with God. He then cuts his throat. The *venticelli* tell the audience that Salieri's efforts failed: he survived his attempted suicide and the public refused to believe he had murdered Mozart. The play ends with Salieri, in a gesture of benediction, telling the audience, "mediocrities everywhere—now and to come—I absolve you all. Amen." He then folds his arms "high across his own breast in a gesture of self-sanctification."

Characters

Audience

Salieri often addresses the audience to gain their support and understanding as the scenes shift back to the play's present. At the beginning of the play, when Salieri asks the members of the audience to be visible to him, the house lights go up so he can see them. He then tells them he is at their service and that he wants them to be his confessors. At the play's end, he warns the audience that they also will feel "the dreadful bite" of their failures, and when they do, Salieri as Patron Saint of Mediocrities will absolve them.

Katherina Cavalieri

Katherina is Salieri's pupil, a "beautiful girl of twenty" who has affairs with Salieri and Mozart. Her part is mute like that of Teresa, Salieri's wife. Salieri is in love with Katherina—"or at least in lust"—but he remains faithful to his wife until he determines that God has betrayed him. She then becomes his mistress. By the end of the play, Katherina appears "fat and feathered like the great song-bird she'd become."

Emperor of Austria

See Joseph II

Ghosts of the Future

See Audience

God

Salieri presents the audience with his subjective vision of God as "an old candle-smoked God in a mulberry robe, staring at the world with dealer's eyes....Those eyes made bargains, real and irreversible." God becomes Salieri's "cunning Enemy," whom he continually tries to block. Salieri's God is unjust, as when he notes:

> You gave me the desire to serve You —which most men do not have— then saw to it the service was shameful in the ears of the server.... You gave me the desire to praise You—which most men do not feel— then made me mute.... You put into me perception of the Incomparable— which most men never know!—then ensured that I would know myself forever mediocre.

Joseph II

Joseph, the brother of Marie Antoinette, is an "adorer of music—provided that it made no demands upon the royal brain." Unfortunately,

Mozart's music often demands too much of him, and, as a result, he is easily influenced by Salieri and others at court to hold Mozart in check.

Little Winds

See Venticelli

Constanze Mozart

See Constanze Weber

Leopold Mozart

Salieri describes Wolfgang's father as "a bad-tempered Salzburg musician who dragged the boy endlessly round Europe, making him play the keyboard blindfolded, with one finger." The audience never meets Leopold, but he makes his presence felt through his son, who is afraid of him. Mozart claims his father is a bitter man who is jealous of his success. He continually tries to control Mozart's actions but for the most part fails. Mozart marries Constanze Weber against his father's wishes and stays in Vienna, living well above his means. Yet psychologically, Leopold has a great influence over his son. When he dies, Mozart falls apart, exclaiming, "How will I go now? In the world. There's no one else. No one who understands the wickedness around. I can't see it.... He watched for me all my life—and I betrayed him." Leopold becomes the solemn ghost in *Don Giovanni,* "a father more accusing than any in opera." Mozart creates a more benevolent version of his father, however, in *The Magic Flute,* where he appears as a high priest,"his hand extended to the world in love." As he dies, Mozart mistakes Salieri for his father and cries out for him as he regresses back to his childhood.

Wolfgang Amadeus Mozart

We see Mozart through Salieri's memory. Salieri does provide some background information on the famous prodigy. He wrote his first symphony at five, his first concerto at four, a full opera at fourteen, and is twenty-five when Salieri meets him. The stage directions introduce him as "a small, pallid, large-eyed man in a showy wig and a showy set of clothes." Mozart is "an extremely restless man, his hands and feet in almost continuous motion, his voice is light and high, and he is possessed of an unforgettable giggle—piercing and infantile." He enjoys ribald jokes and bathroom humor, a quality which disgusts and angers Salieri, who insists his own virtuous nature deserves to be blessed by God.

Mozart has a love/hate relationship with his father, whom he fears but also respects. He desperately needs his father's approval and so reincarnates him in his compositions. The *venticelli* tell Salieri that Mozart is "wildly extravagant" and lives way beyond his means. His outbursts in public have become "embarrassing." He "makes scenes" and thus often "makes enemies." Yet, Salieri insists that God has chosen him as his voice, as evident in his exquisite music. Mozart comments on his role as artist and his goal to make

> ...a sound entirely new.... I bet you that's how God hears the world. Millions of sounds ascending at once and mixing in His ear to become an unending music, unimaginable to us. That's our job... we composers: to combine the inner minds of him and him and her and her—the thoughts of chambermaids and court composers —and turn the audience into God.

By the end of the play, we see how circumstances broke Mozart and he soon dies.

Count Franz Orsini-Rosenberg

Director of the Imperial Opera, Orsini-Rosenberg is "plump and supercilious." He clashes with Mozart about the appropriateness of his music and vows to take his revenge when Mozart gets the emperor's approval.

Antonio Salieri

Court composer to the Emperor of Austria, Salieri is "the most successful young musician in the city of musicians," yet he is also consumed with envy of Mozart's prodigious musical talents. He finds himself mediocre by comparison. Providing a brief portrait of his background, he explains that his

parents were

...provincial subjects of the Austrian Empire.... Their notion of God was a superior Habsburg emperor.... All they required of Him was to protect commerce, and keep them forever preserved in mediocrity. My own requirements were very different. I wanted 'Fame.'... Yet only in one especial way.

Media Adaptations

- An overwhelmingly popular film version was released in 1984. *Amadeus* was directed by Milos Forman and starred F. Murray Abraham as Salieri and Tom Hulce as Mozart. Shaffer wrote the screenplay. This film is available in VHS and DVD formats.

- A television version appeared in Romania, directed by Radu Cernescu and starring Razvan Vasilescu as Mozart and Radu Beligan as Salieri. The production used Shaffer's play for the script.

Music! Absolute music....Already when I was ten a spray of sounded notes would make me dizzy almost to falling. By twelve, I was stumbling about under the poplar trees humming my arias and anthems to the Lord. My one desire was to join all the composers who had celebrated His glory through the long Italian past.

When Mozart's talents clearly surpass his own, he feels as if God is mocking him. As a result, Salieri declares war against God "through His preferred Creature—Mozart ... in the waging of which, of course, the Creature had to be destroyed." Salieri eventually contributes to Mozart's destruction, yet admits that he did not escape God's punishment. He had fame, but it was for what he knew to be "absolutely worthless."

Salieri, however, is tenacious. He decides, "I did not live on earth to be His joke for eternity. I will be remembered... if not in fame, then infamy." When he falsely confesses to poisoning Mozart, he insists "for the rest of time whenever men say

Mozart with love, they will say Salieri with loathing.... I am going to be immortal after all." Yet he is again thwarted. His suicide attempt fails, and no one believes his confession. At the end of the play, he is enveloped in his bitterness as he addresses the audience as the "Patron Saint of Mediocrities."

Stanzi

See Constanze Weber

Baron Gottfried Van Swieten

The emperor's prefect of the Imperial Library, Van Swieten is "cultivated and serious," and an ardent Freemason. He is known, because of his enthusiasm for old-fashioned music, as "Lord Fugue." Van Swieten defends "passionately" the traditional subjects of the opera because "they represent the eternal in us. Opera is here to ennoble us.... It is an aggrandizing art. It celebrates the eternal in man and ignores the ephemeral. The goddess in woman and not the laundress." He becomes outraged when he discovers that Mozart has put the Mason's rituals into what he deems "a vulgar show." As a result, he sees to it that Mozart gets no more work. After Mozart dies, Van Swieten pays only for a pauper's funeral and buries Mozart along with twenty other corpses in an unmarked grave.

Venticelli

The two *venticelli* are "purveyors of fact, rumor, and gossip throughout the play." They speak rapidly, especially in the opening scene, which "has the air of a fast and dreadful overture." They sometimes speak to Salieri, sometimes to each other, and sometimes directly to the audience. Salieri explains their usefulness to him when he notes,"the secret of successful living in a large city is always to know to the minute what is being done behind your back." The *venticelli* always speak "with the urgency of men who have ever been first with the news." They open the play with the information that "the whole city is talking day and night" about Salieri and his claim to have poisoned Mozart.

Count Johann Von Strack

Von Strack is the groom of the Imperial Chamber in the emperor's court. He is "stiff and proper" and "official to his collarbone." He, along with Van Swieten and Orsini-Rosenberg, advise the emperor in the play on musical matters that involve the court.

Constanze Weber

Mozart marries Constanze, his landlady's daughter, "a pretty girl with high spirits." She often quarrels with Mozart about his infidelities and his father, but she supports his work. She offers herself to Salieri in an effort to help her husband gain employment. After Mozart's death, Constanze marries and retires to Salzburg, Mozart's birthplace, "to become the pious Keeper of his Shrine." In her role as Mozart's widow, she presents herself as "a pillar of rectitude."

Themes

Beauty

Salieri finds absolute beauty in music and so asks God to grant him the gift of artistic inspiration in his compositions. He came to appreciate the beauty of music at a young age, noting,"when I was ten a spray of sounded notes would make me dizzy almost to falling." Unfortunately, he finds this absolute beauty only in Mozart's compositions. When Mozart plays, he confesses that he hears the "voice of God," and he responds with such delight that it makes him tremble.

God and Religion

Connected with Salieri's pursuit of absolute beauty is his search for spiritual meaning, for a supreme logic in the universe. Salieri makes an ironic Faustian bargain in the play. (Faust, a magician and alchemist in German legend, sells his soul to the devil in exchange for power and knowledge.) Instead of constructing a bargain with the devil to attain an ideal, he forms one with God. He longs "to join all the composers who had celebrated His glory through the long Italian past" and so implores God, "let me be a composer... in return, I will live with virtue...and I will honor You with much music all the days of my life." When he decides that God has accepted his bargain, Salieri promises to be His servant for life. Salieri explains, "I was born a pair of ears and nothing else. It is only through hearing music that I know God exists. Only through writing music that I could worship."

Creativity and Imagination

Salieri searches for a supreme logic in the granting of the gifts of creativity and imagination. He is sure that artistic inspiration and talent are gifts given by God only to those who are worthy of them.

Duty and Responsibility

Salieri tries to prove his worthiness through a devotion to duty and responsibility. Although he has been tempted to commit adultery, especially with his pupil Katherina Cavalieri, he restrains himself and redoubles his commitment to the celebration of God through music. Salieri also shows his devotion through his philanthropic activities, as in his support of young, impoverished composers.

However, he turns his back on his noble commitments when he feels that God has favored Mozart over him. In response, he determines that no longer will he deny himself his desires and so takes Katherina as his mistress. Seeing no tangible reward, he also drops his philanthropic activities. Finally, he determines to take revenge by destroying Mozart.

Betrayal

When Salieri decides that God has granted the gift of inspiration to Mozart, whom he deems unworthy, he feels betrayed, claiming that God has been actively toying with Salieri's devotion and desires. He concludes that God has been taunting him by giving him the desire to serve and to praise God, and the ability to recognize true art, only after ensuring his own mediocrity. Salieri's God cruelly flaunts the "spiteful, sniggering, conceited, infantine" Mozart in front of Salieri as one of His chosen to point out Salieri's inferiority and thus humiliate him. Salieri is convinced that Mozart has become God's incarnation. The final irony, one that Salieri uses to help him destroy Mozart, is that Salieri is the only person at that time who can recognize Mozart's greatness.

Justice and Injustice

As a result of what he considers to be God's injustice, Salieri decides to exact his own form of justice regarding Mozart, even though he risks damnation. A bitter Salieri warns God that he now considers Him an enemy, and so with his "last breath" he will try to block God's plan for Mozart's "worldly advancement." After reading Mozart's manuscripts and appreciating the exquisite beauty of his work, Salieri confesses that his life then acquired this "terrible and thrilling purpose." He hints at his plan to destroy Mozart when he insists that he will now engage in "a battle to the end" with God and that Mozart will be "the battleground."

Ironically though, according to Salieri, God exacted his own justice, perhaps in response to Salieri's treatment of Mozart. Salieri concludes that God constructed an intricate and cruel plan to punish him: first, He (God) ensured that Salieri would enjoy the recognition and appreciation of a public who was not capable of recognizing true art. Then, that recognition would be taken away from him and replaced with the public's growing appreciation for Mozart's music. Gradually, as "Mozart's music sounded louder and louder through the world," his would "fade completely, till no one played it at all."

Topics for Further Study

- Research the biographies of Mozart and Salieri. Was Shaffer's portrayal of the two composers and their relationship accurate?

- Define existentialism and discover

how playwrights have incorporated this theme in their plays. What existential elements do you find in *Amadeus*?

- Read Shaffer's *Equus* and compare its themes to those of *Amadeus*. What differences do you find? What similarities do you find? Can you find a pattern in both plays?

- Listen to the pieces by Mozart that are mentioned in the play, especially the ones Salieri hears during a live performance or in his head. How does the music reinforce the play's themes?

Style

Narration

The play is structured like a deathbed confession, similar to Monticello's in Edgar Allan Poe's short story "The Cask of Amontillado." The play opens after the main events have occurred and with one of the main characters, Antonio Salieri, speaking to the audience as an old man. Salieri frequently addresses the audience directly, sometimes in an aside, during the course of the play to gain support and understanding. This self-conscious, expression-istic device not only provides the audience with useful information; it also allows them a glimpse of Salieri's inner thoughts and emotions. When Salieri speaks to the audience, the other characters often "freeze" and the soundtrack stops. The *venticelli,* or the "Little Winds," sometimes speak directly to the audience as they relate important information about the events surrounding Salieri's relationship with Mozart. The *venticelli* also provide Salieri with useful information about Mozart's activities and the public's response to both composers.

Salieri's narration frames the play, which opens and closes with a focus on Salieri as a bitter old man, lamenting the loss of his fame and the overwhelming appreciation of Mozart's work. The older Salieri also appears at the middle of the play to offer a commentary on the main plot details surrounding his relationship with Mozart.

Point of View

Shaffer tells the story of the relationship between Mozart and Salieri from Salieri's subjective point of view. While other characters in the play often substantiate Salieri's opinion of Mozart's character, especially when he challenges the composer's petulance and immaturity, they do not validate his portrayal of God's motives and behavior. Salieri's God is "an old candle-smoked God in a mulberry robe, staring at the world with dealer's eyes"—a vision he takes from a painting he saw as a child. Salieri cannot admit to any responsibility for his artistic shortcomings and so must blame God for them. He insists that when he was young, God promised to grant him the gift of music. When He does not live up to this promise, He becomes Salieri's "cunning Enemy," whom Salieri continually tries to block. Salieri's God proves unjust to him after, he claims, God gave Salieri the desire to serve Him through music, but then "saw to it the service was shameful in the ears of the server" and gave him the ability to recognize greatness while acknowledging his own mediocrity.

Salieri's God is also pitiless, insisting that He (God) does not need Salieri because He has Mozart. When Salieri decides God has also turned his back on Mozart, Salieri tells the artist that God will not help or love him, for "God does not love. He can only use.... He cares nothing for whom He uses; nothing for whom He denies."

Symbol

The title of the play, *Amadeus,* translates into "God's love" and thus becomes ironically symbolic in the play. Salieri continually tries to gain recognition of God's love for him, especially since his "one desire was to join all the composers who had celebrated His glory through the long Italian past." However, he sees an expression of God's love only in Mozart's music, which baffles him and drives him to the verge of madness. When he hears one of Mozart's compositions, Salieri confesses, "it seemed to me that I had heard a voice of God—and that it issued from a creature whose own voice I had also heard—and it was the voice of an obscene child!"

Shaffer also uses music symbolically in the play. His inclusion of Mozart's most lyrical and stirring passages illustrates "God's voice" in the music, especially when juxtaposed with Salieri's more pedestrian pieces. Shaffer also uses the music to allow the audience to glimpse Salieri's inner turmoil. For example, when Salieri reads the manuscripts Constanze brings him, he hears Mozart's swelling music and "staggers" forward "like a man caught in a tumbling and violent sea." When the drums "crash," Salieri echoes the emotion of the piece as he drops the manuscripts and "falls senseless to the ground." Shaffer directs, "At the same second the music explodes into a long, echoing, distorted boom, signifying some dreadful annihilation." At this climactic point, Salieri's dream of becoming God's chosen has been shattered.

Historical Context

Mozart

In the twentieth century, Wolfgang Amadeus Mozart's reputation grew considerably. His works, which include a variety of forms from chamber music to symphonies and operas, have been heralded for their classical grace, technical perfection, and melodic beauty.

Shaffer's play, *Amadeus,* records several details of Mozart's life. Mozart was a child prodigy who started composing before he was five. A year later, his father began taking him and his talented sister to play for the aristocracy in Europe. In 1781, he relocated to Vienna and married Constanze Weber against his father's wishes. The newly weds had financial difficulties when Mozart could not find suitable employment. While his work was often applauded during his lifetime, audiences were sometimes critical of the demands his innovations placed on them. He also clashed with the emperor's court over issues of artistic freedom. Eventually, he was appointed chamber musician and court composer to Joseph II, but the paltry salary he earned did not ease his financial troubles. He gained public acclaim claim for *The Magic Flute,* but the work's references to the secret rituals of the Freemasons lost him the support of one of his most ardent defenders, Baron von Swieten. Mozart worked on his final piece, the *Requiem Mass,* with the sense that it would be played at his own funeral. He died, however, before he could complete it and was buried, unceremoniously, in an unmarked, mass grave.

Compare & Contrast

- **1781:** Joseph II is Emperor of Austria

  1918: The Austrian monarchy is abolished as a result of the political turmoil of World War I.

  Today: Austria is a prosperous and independent country.

- **1781:** Music flourishes in eighteenth-century Austria, due in large part to the strong support and patronage of Joseph II.

  Today: Many American congressmen support massive cuts in subsidies for the arts.

Mozart and Salieri

Other artists have created works based on the rumor that Salieri may have murdered Mozart. In 1830, Alexander Pushkin wrote a tragedy entitled *Envy,* which he later renamed *Mozart and Salieri*. In

1897, Nikolay Rimsky-Korsakov based his opera, *Mozart and Salieri,* on Pushkin's short dramatic sketch, which focuses on Salieri's envy and his subsequent poisoning of Mozart, who dies playing his *Requiem* on the piano.

Freemasons

The Order of the Freemasons is a secret fraternal order also known as the Free and Accepted Masons, or Ancient Free and Accepted Masons. The Freemasons has over six million members worldwide and is the largest secret society in the world. No central authority governs the Masons. Each national group, called a grand lodge, is a self-governing body.

The Masonic rituals and ceremonies are elaborate and symbolic. They often employ the tools of stonemasonry—the plumb, square, level, and compass—and use as an allegorical backdrop the events surrounding the building of King Solomon's Temple. Masons are expected to believe in a Supreme Being and to read a holy book designated by the lodge. All members are sworn to secrecy concerning the order's ceremonies and rituals.

Some scholars argue that the order emerged from the English and Scottish stonemason fraternities and cathedral workmen in the early Middle Ages. Traces of the order have been found in Great Britain in the fourteenth century. Other historians speculate that evidence of the order can be found in antiquity. The order flourished worldwide after the formation of the English Grand Lodge in London in 1717. Famous freemasons include Voltaire, Joseph Haydn, Johann von Goethe, and Benjamin Franklin.

The various productions of *Amadeus* have received mixed reviews from the critics but overwhelmingly enthusiastic support from audiences. Peter Shaffer notes in his introduction to the play that when it opened at the National Theatre of Great Britain in November 1979, "it constituted the single greatest success enjoyed by this celebrated institution since its founding." Since its initial performance, the play's popularity has spread to Broadway, with runs of more than one thousand performances each, and several European stages. Bernard Levin, in a review for the *Times* (London), comments on audience response: "those who go to [*Amadeus*] prepared to understand what it is about will have an experience that far transcends even its considerable value as drama."

Those critics who find "considerable value" in *Amadeus* include Roland Gelatt, who writes in the *Saturday Review* that the play "gives heartening evidence that there is still room for the play of ideas." Werner Huber and Hubert Zapt, in their article for *Modern Drama,* praise the structure of the play, arguing that it

> can be seen as a highly sophisticated
> process of interpretive interaction
> between the stage and the audience,
> in which Salieri as the self-confessed
> murderer of Mozart is the central

mediator.... There is a degree of thematic and structural complexity to *Amadeus,* which makes it, beyond its sensational popularity, a dramatic masterpiece in its own right. The play is an artistic success not only for its technical refinement (i.e., the exploitation to the full of various theatrical forms) and dramatic richness, but for the intellectual brilliance with which the theme is handled, giving the play its specifically modern appeal.

Some critics, however, find fault with Shaffer's characterization of Mozart. Robert Brustein, in the *New Republic,* insists that "at the same time that the central character—a second-rate *kapellmeister* named Antonio Salieri—is plotting against the life and reputation of a superior composer named Wolfgang Amadeus Mozart, a secondary playwright named Peter Shaffer is reducing this genius, one of the greatest artists of all time, to the level of a simpering, braying ninny." In *Opera News,* C. J. Gianakaris refutes those who question the truthfulness of Mozart's characterization, commenting, "Shaffer takes almost no liberties with historical fact about Mozart and his times, except where Salieri the man is concerned." Daniel R. Jones, in *Comparative Drama,* explains, "Mozart's animal play-acting, his word-play, his financial difficulties, his marriage to a child-like wife, and his domineering father are well documented in the biographies, Mozart's three volumes of correspondence, and in the correspondence of relatives."

Others criticize Shaffer's characterization of Salieri. In his article for *Comparative Drama,* Michael Hinden, for example, condemns Salieri's overwhelming pessimism as he "abandons his quest for union with divinity and becomes the antagonist of God, setting himself against the Deity in personal confrontation and defiance." Benedict Nightingale, in his review for the *New Statesman,* complains of Salieri's "implausibility." He comments that Salieri

> is thought to have schemed to Mozart's disadvantage, and, in his senility, is said to have claimed to have poisoned him. From these hints and rumours Shaffer manufactures a blend of Iago and Faust, much at odds with the historical Salieri, whose conventional efforts were as triumphant as Mozart's musical adventures were neglected, and therefore had no motive for murder.

Amadeus won five Tonys for its New York performances, including a Tony for best drama of the 1980 season. The popularity of the play ensured the success of the 1984 film version, which received nominations for eleven Oscars, winning eight including best picture, best director, and best actor.

What Do I Read Next?

- *Classical Music: The Era of Haydn, Mozart, and Beethoven: Norton Introduction to Music History,* by Philip G. Downs (1992), presents a useful study of Mozart and his contemporaries.

- Shaffer's play *Equus,* produced in 1973, presents another exploration of two men of widely differing personalities linked by a common spiritual bond.

- In *Mozart in Revolt: Strategies of Resistance, Mischief and Deception* (1999), David P. Schroeder examines the letters Mozart and his father wrote to each other. He discovers important information about the personality of each man as well as their relationship to each other.

- *1791: Mozart's Last Year,* written by H. C. Robbins Landon and M. C. Landon (1999), explores the controversial last year of Mozart's life and the rumors of Salieri's involvement in his death.

- Jean-Paul Sartre's play *Nausea* (1938) deals with existential themes as *Amadeus* does. In Sartre's play, the main characters must cope with a God-abandoned universe and turn to art in an effort to alleviate their sense of meaninglessness.

Sources

Brustein, Robert, Review in *New Republic,* January 17, 1981.

Gelatt, Roland, "Peter Shaffer's *Amadeus:* A Controversial Hit," in *Saturday Review,* November 1980, pp. 11-14.

Gianakaris, C. J., Review in *Opera News,* Vol. 46, February 27, 1982.

Hinden, Michael, "Trying to Like Shaffer," in *Comparative Drama,* Vol. 19, Spring 1985, pp. 14-29.

Huber, Werner, and Hubert Zapf, "On the Structure of Peter Shaffer's *Amadeus,"* in *Modern Drama,* Vol. 27, No. 3, September 1984, pp. 299-313.

Jones, Daniel R., "Peter Shaffer's Continued Quest for God in *Amadeus,"* in *Comparative Drama,* Vol. 21, No. 2, Summer 1987, pp. 145-155.

Kauffmann, Stanley, Review in *Saturday Review,* February 1981, pp. 78-79.

Levin, Bernard, Review in *Times* (London), January 9, 1985.

MacMurraugh-Kavanagh, M. K., *Peter Shaffer: Theatre and Drama,* MacMillan Press, 1998.

Nightingale, Benedict,"Obscene Child," in *New Statesman,* Vol. 98, No. 2538, November 1979, p. 735.

Further Reading

Chambers, Colin, "Psychic Energy," in *Plays and Players,* Vol. 27, No. 5, February 1980, pp. 11-13.

> Chambers includes comments from Shaffer on his plays, including *Amadeus*.

Connell, Brian, "The Two Sides of Theatre's Agonized Perfectionist," in *Times* (London), April 28, 1980, p. 18.

> Connell interviews Shaffer on several topics including his literary development and the structure of his plays.

Taylor, John Russell, *Peter Shaffer,* Longman Group, 1974.

> Taylor analyzes Shaffer's use of language in his plays.

Toynbee, Polly, Review, in *Spectator,* Vol. 243, No. 7896, November 10, 1979, pp. 29-30.

> Toynbee comments on the structure of *Amadeus*. She praises the play's opening premise but faults what she considers its overlong second act.

Printed by BoD™in Norderstedt, Germany